RABBITS

MICHAELA MILLER

Contents

Words in bold, **like this**, are explained in the glossary on page 23.

Wild ones

Rabbits come in all shapes and sizes, from the big Flemish giant to the small Netherland dwarf. But whatever the size and colour, they all come from wild rabbits.

baby wild rabbits

For a long time rabbits were kept just for food. About 400 years ago people started to keep them as pets.

RABBIT FACT

Rabbits like to be with other rabbits. In the wild they live in groups.

3

The rabbit for you

Rabbits need lots of care and attention. Before you get a rabbit, talk about it for a long time with your family.

lop-eared Chinchilla rabbit

RABBIT FACT

Smaller rabbits like Polish, Dutch and Netherland dwarfs are usually better ones to choose.

Big rabbits like Flemish giants or Chinchilla gigantas are not ones to choose, unless you are big and strong yourself. They can weigh quite a lot and are quite a handful.

Where to find your rabbit

Animal shelters are often looking for good homes for rabbits. Ask your friends and local vet if they know anyone with young rabbits. Do not get a rabbit from anywhere that looks dirty.

lop-eared rabbit in a shelter

You can also buy rabbits from **breeders**. A vet could let you know about local breeders. A good one will let you ask lots of questions and will check that their rabbits are going to good homes.

angora rabbit

Long-haired rabbits like angoras need brushing every day.

A healthy rabbit

Choose a rabbit between nine and twelve weeks old that looks lively and healthy. Avoid rabbits with runny noses and signs of **diarrhoea.**

RABBIT FACT

Pet rabbits which are well looked after can live up to eight years.

Your rabbit should have bright clear eyes, a sleek glossy coat, clean teeth which are not too long and very clean ears. It should not have any cuts, lumps or rashes.

Safe hands

Always hold your rabbit properly. This will help it trust you. Start by turning it to face you.

Now put one hand on the **scruff** of its neck and the other hand around its rump.

Lift the rabbit towards you. Then draw your arms in so your rabbit rests closely and safely against your body.

RABBIT FACT

If your rabbit starts to struggle, it's not very happy. Put it down gently on a non-slip surface.

Feeding time

Feed your rabbit two small meals at the same times each day. Lettuce, dandelions, grass, vegetables, fruit, good quality hay and 'rabbit pellets' should all be on the menu.

RABBIT FACT

Rabbits need heavy feeding bowls. They will tip light ones over.

Keep a full **drip-fed water bottle** with a stainless steel spout in your rabbit's home at all times. Rabbits need a small block of wood to chew on as well. This helps to keep their teeth the right length.

Home sweet home

Most pet shop rabbit houses are too small. Your rabbit house should be at least 150 cm long, 60 cm wide and 60 cm high. It should be split into two halves – one with a strong wire-mesh door and one with a solid door. The house should be about 80 cm off the ground.

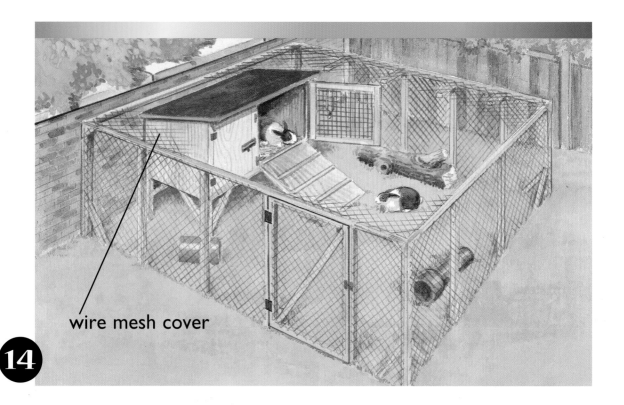

wire mesh cover

Rabbits need a large space to hop about and graze. Put the house on a piece of grass with a strong fence around and cover with mesh to stop cats getting in. A ramp should lead from the ground to the rabbit house so they can come and go as they please.

rabbit in a burrow

RABBIT FACT

If the fence is not sunk into the ground the rabbits will burrow out.

Keeping clean

Your rabbit house will need a five-cm-layer of **peat**, cat **litter**, natural wood fibre chippings or shavings on the floor. Cover this with a very deep layer of shredded paper or straw. Clean the whole house twice a week.

RABBIT FACT

Wet litter and droppings must be removed every day to keep a rabbit house clean.

Rabbits can use **litter trays** and be house-trained to live indoors. Try putting a few droppings and some paper soaked in its **urine** where you want it to go to the toilet.

At the vet's

Pet rabbits need to go to the vet for a check-up at least once a year. They should also be **vaccinated** against **myxomatosis** and other nasty diseases.

Check with a vet if your rabbit doesn't seem well. If it does not want to eat, is finding breathing difficult or has sticky ears, eyes, nose, mouth or tail area then it needs to see a vet at once.

RABBIT FACT

Flystrike can kill rabbits. It starts when flies lay eggs around your rabbit's tail. Check your rabbit's bottom every day in warm weather.

No more babies

Don't let your rabbits have babies. They could have as many as eight babies per **litter** and two to three litters a year. It would be impossible for you to find homes for them all.

mother with her babies

RABBIT FACT

Rabbits and guinea pigs can live together if they are introduced when they are very young.

Keep rabbits of the same sex together. But male rabbits kept together need to be **neutered** to stop them fighting. Always ask your vet for advice on neutering and how to keep rabbits together.

21

A note from the RSPCA

Pets are lots of fun and can end up being our best friends. These animal friends need very special treatment – plenty of kindness, a good home, the right food and lots of attention.

This book helps you to understand what your pet needs. It also shows you how you can play an important part in looking after your pet. But the adults in your family must be in overall charge of any family pet. This means that they should get advice from a vet and read about how to give your pet the best care.

Why not become a member of the RSPCA's Animal Action Club. You'll receive a membership card, badge, stickers and magazine. To find out how to join, write to RSPCA Animal Action Club, Causeway, Horsham, West Sussex RH12 1HG.

FURTHER READING

22

The Queen's nose **by Dick King-Smith**
Revenge of the rabbit **by Rose Impey**

Glossary

animal shelters also known as centres or homes. There are lots of these shelters all around the country which look after unwanted pets and try to find them new homes. The RSPCA has about 50 animal centres in England and Wales.

burrow dig underground. An underground home for wild rabbits

drip-fed water bottle a bottle which is specially made so that the water comes out drip by drip

litter group of new born rabbits. Special gravel for a litter tray.

litter tray a box where the rabbit can go to the toilet.

myxomatosis a disease carried by the rabbit flea, which can kill rabbits. Rabbits can be vaccinated to protect them

neutered an operation to stop rabbits from having babies

peat soil used to line the bottom of a rabbit house

scruff loose skin around the back of the neck

urine rabbit's wee

vaccinated to be injected by a vet to stop rabbits catching diseases

Index

First published in Great Britain by Heinemann Library, Halley Court, Jordan Hill, Oxford OX2 8EJ, a division of Reed Educational and Professional Publishing Ltd

OXFORD FLORENCE PRAGUE MADRID ATHENS MELBOURNE AUCKLAND KUALA LUMPUR SINGAPORE TOKYO IBADAN NAIROBI KAMPALA

JOHANNESBURG GABORONE PORTSMOUTH NH CHICAGO MEXICO CITY SAO PAULO

Designed by Nicki Wise and Lisa Nutt

Illustrations by Michael Strand

Colour reproduction by Colourpath, London

Printed in Hong Kong / China

01 00 99 98

10 9 8 7 6 5 4 3 2

ISBN 0 431 03371 4

This title is also available in hardback edition.

British Library Cataloguing in Publication Data

Miller, Michaela

Rabbits. - (Pets)

1.Rabbits - Juvenile literature

I .Title II . Royal Society for the Prevention of Cruelty to Animals

636.9'322

Acknowledgements

The Publishers would like to thank the following for permission to reproduce photographs.

Ardea/ pp20 John Daniels; Dave Bradford pp10-13, 17, 21; Bruce Coleman Ltd p7 Fritz Prenzel; OSF/ pp6 Avril Ramage, 15 G I Bernard; RSPCA/ pp2 William S Paton, 3 Colin Carver, 4 E A Janes, 5, 18, 19 Tim Sambrook, 8 A M Glue, 9 Angela Hampton.

Cover photographs reproduced with permission of: RSPCA; Dave Bradford

Our thanks to Ann Head and her pets; Pippa Bush, Bill Swan and Jim Philips for their help in the preparation of this book; Pets Mart for the kind loan of equipment; the children of Oaklands Infants School.

Every effort has been made to contact copyright holders of any material reproduced in this book. Any omissions will be rectified in subsequent printings if notice is given to the Publisher.